Copyright © 2017 LaVerne Jackson-Harvey

All rights reserved. No parts of this book may be reproduced in any form or used without the permission from the author.

The Author can be reached at
laverne.harvey@yahoo.com for speaking engagement requests,
or visit her website at www.lavernejharvey.com if you would like to purchase additional copies of this book.

ISBN-13:
978-0990911937 (LaVerne Jackson-Harvey)

ISBN-10:
0990911934

EBONY THOUGHTS:
POEMS FROM A CULTURAL PERSPECTIVE

Ebony Thoughts

Introduction to Ebony Thoughts: Poem From A Cultural Perspective

It is my pleasure to share with you my third book of poetry entitled, *Ebony Thoughts: Poems From A Cultural Perspective*. This book highlights poetry from a diverse perspective and life experiences. It addresses issues that affect African American life and culture. Written through the lens of an African American author, it touches upon issues of race, injustices, inspiration, family, and current events.

My personal and professional backgrounds include growing up during the Jim Crow South Era, segregation, attending a Historically Black College and predominately White colleges, working in rural and urban environments with students from K-12 to college, and teaching at the college level. My experiences are diverse varying from all angles of the spectrum. Many of the poems in this collection are based on my life experiences at different stages in my life. Included in this collection are the poems Dot Drowning in a Sea of White, Black Excellence, Don't Break Their Spirit, A Day of National Pride, All Lives

Matter But Not Equally, Educate Not Incarcerate, Black Girls Lift Your Head High, and Black Child, to name a few.

I have published two additional books of poetry and a children's book. The first book of poetry, Life Circumstances: *Do Not Let Life Circumstances Limit Your Outcome,* addresses many events in life we all experience. The second book of poetry, *A Ray of Hope: Poems of Inspiration*, will inspire you to hope for a better future. In my children's book, *Ruth and Her Hoots*, I share life lessons my mom taught her eleven children about overcoming obstacles and the power of love and fam ily.

It is my hope that you will reflect and enjoy the life lessons shared through *Ebony Thoughts: Poems From A Cultural Perspective.* I would like to thank my family and friends for their encouragement and support in writing this book of poetry.

Ebony Thoughts

TABLE OF CONTENTS

INTRODUCTION TO EBONY THOUGHTS: POEMS FROM A CULTURAL PERSPECTIVE	3
BLACK EXCELLENCE	8
DAY OF NATIONAL PRIDE	10
ALL LIVES MATTERS...BUT IT'S NOT EQUAL	12
DOT DROWNING IN A	14
SEA OF WHITE	14
WHY DOES IT HURT SO BAD?	17
TIME - MAKE EVERY SECOND COUNT	20
MAMA'S BOY	21
EDUCATE NOT INCARCERATE	23
RISE	25
THE MASK	26
THROUGH THE EYES OF BABIES	27
A SEASON OF HOPE	28
THE MORE THINGS CHANGE THE MORE THEY STAY THE SAME	31
FIND YOUR WINGS	34
BLACK GIRLS LIFT YOUR HEAD HIGH	35
THE BOX	36
YOUNG PEOPLE WAKE UP	37
A RAY OF HOPE	39
WHAT'S RACE GOT TO DO WITH IT?	40
WE ARE OUR OWN WORST ENEMY	42
PROUD BLACK WOMAN	44
THE ALPHA WOMEN	47

Ebony Thoughts

A MOTHER'S TOUCH	49
SEE THE BEAUTY IN ME	51
IN HER SHOES	52
BLACK CHILD	54
CLAFLIN UNIVERSITY-YOU ARE ONE OF A KIND	56
NOT GOOD ENOUGH	61
FINDING OUR VOICES	62
DREAM THE POSSIBLE	63
PAIN	64
SELF DOUBT CAN HURT	65
STRIVE FOR EXCELLENCE	67
BEHIND THE CURTAIN	68
WHY ME?	69
COUNT YOUR BLESSINGS	71
THE HISTORICAL PLIGHT OF THE STRONG BLACK MAN	73
OBAMA-YES YOU CAN	78
IMPULSE	81
KEEP THE FAITH	82
TOXIC PEOPLE	84
WHY TEACH? WHY NOT!!!	85
DO NOT LET LIFE'S CIRCUMSTANCES LIMIT YOUR OUTCOME	88
FIGHT EVERYDAY WE MUST	90
DON'T BREAK THEIR SPIRIT	91
BARRY BONDS-GO 756	94
HERE WE GO AGAIN	98

Ebony Thoughts

BEING AN AFRICAN AMERICAN STUDENT IN THE
TWENTIETH FIRST CENTURY   102
IT'S YOUR CHOICE: HATE OR HOPE   106
MICHAEL JACKSON: A JOURNEY OF GREATNESS   109
ABOUT THE AUTHOR   111

Black Excellence

Black Excellence defines us
Despite injustices, racism, slavery, and
The attempt to dehumanize a race of people
We are still standing tall

Despite attempts in the past to not educate our
ancestors, to threaten those who dared to make a
difference, despite shackles
We rose over the hill to see our future, to see the
light, to see freedom

As a people, we are strong, beautiful, Black, proud,
and achievers
We have made great contributions to this country,
To this society, and all over the world

We must continue to stand tall
To strengthen others so they do not fall
Into the trap of not believing in themselves
Not loving themselves
Not embracing their God-given gifts

We must propel them to dream
We must educate them on our magnificent history
and our long list of accomplishments
in all areas of academia
Black Excellence recognizes the brilliance, the grit,
the growth, achievements, and the strength of a
strong, resilient, and proud people

Ebony Thoughts

I was so touched by the commemoration of the National Museum of African American History and Culture and hearing our first African American President, President Barack Obama and other dignitaries' remarks at the event. I felt so much pride as an African American knowing this was a long time coming. I could feel the souls of our ancestors saying, well done. After seeing the event on television and being so touched I wrote the poem, "A Day of National Pride".

Day of National Pride

This is a day of national pride
September 24, 2016
For the African American culture and America
The inauguration of the National Museum of
African American History and Culture on the
National Mall
This has been a long-time coming
When we look at the history of our culture
The good, bad, and the ugly
This is a beautiful moment in time
Seeing the first African American President,
President Barack Obama, so eloquently speaking at
This momentous event
The pride of the people
We can rejoice on the accomplishment of our
people
When we look at the history of African Americans
We know we are a strong people

Despite the injustices, inequality, slavery, and
The hate of a people
We are still standing
Despite unjustified killing of our Black men,
women, and children
We are still standing
Despite our ancestors dying for justice
We are still standing
Despite being treated less than a human being
We are still standing
Despite our continuous struggles
For justice and equality

Ebony Thoughts

We are still standing
 Despite the negative political atmosphere, the open display of hate,
The failure of the justice system to protect all people
We are still standing

I know our ancestors are beaming with pride
To see this moment of time
To know through their sacrifices
Changes are being made
To see a ray of hope
That their sacrifices have made this moment possible
We have a long way to go to correct many of the injustices
But as African Americans
We can bask in the moment and
Be proud of the accomplishments of our people
This is a start of what needs to happen in the future
Let's continue to lift our voices and take action for change
Let's rejoice on this day of pride

All Lives Matters…But It's Not Equal

All Lives Matters but history has shown
That treatment of lives from different cultures is not equal, from our past to the future
Black lives have always been regarded with less value
We were not seen as a full human being
But counted as 3/5 of a person in our history

Our men were hung and treated less than a dog
Our women were raped without total regard for their feelings
Our children were taken from their parents and sold to the highest bidder
The family unit held on by a string
Black lives had to endure the Jim Crow Laws
Our ancestors were killed trying to get an education and making a better life for their children
They were forced to work from sunrise to sunset at the demand of their slave owners
This included men, women, and children

Through our strong foundation
Our religion, and our determination to not let our spirits be broken but continue to fight against injustices
We Are Still Standing

Our Black men were killed for anything including looking at a White woman
They were found guilty of crimes without evidence

Ebony Thoughts

They were guilty until proven innocent, instead of innocent until proven guilty
Our strong Black men fought for their freedom despite threats against their lives
They fought to be with and provide for their wife and children and to keep their family intact
They were feared by their slave owners because
They would not go down without a struggle

When we say, all lives matter we must look at the Good, Bad, and Ugly of our history
We have to look at slavery, White privilege, discrimination, inequality, the dual system of justice, the KKK and other hate groups, racism, voting rights suppression, the use of unnecessary force and the killing of our Black men at the hand of law enforcement officers, health care, crime, unequal educational opportunities, unemployment, gun rights, equal pay, politics, laws, disrespect of our first Black President, unequal coverage by the news media, oppression, lynching, poverty, to name a few, to see where injustice exists

We once again must fight for justice caused by the injustices that exist
Let it be known that "Black Lives Do Matter"
But history shows that it's not equal

Dot Drowning in a Sea of White

DOT-Black people and people of color who wear the badge of color
White-dominant or majority race that makes many decisions that affect or impact all
People including the dot
The impacts of their decisions are not always equal
As a Black person in America
You sometimes feel you are drowning in a sea of white

Your perspective is not relevant
Your culture is not important
Your people viewed as an inferior race
Your children and people are not seen as equal, always having to prove yourself
Even when you have more experience and more education
Your voice is not heard, is ignored, and many times silenced

A dot is circular, on-going, continuous
A sea is open, encumbers much, turbulent, stormy, and volatile affecting the outcomes
Of its inhabitants
Many times, our students are the dot in the sea of white, drowning

They need teachers who see their potential
They need teachers who see them as an asset not a deficit

Ebony Thoughts

They need teachers who teach them, not fear them
They need teachers who set high expectations and not expect them to fail
They need teachers who embrace their differences and not feel threatened
They need teachers to see the brilliance in them

They need teachers who respect their culture and acknowledge its existence
They need highly qualified teachers who can bring their expertise and skills in the
Classroom challenging them to stretch their knowledge
They need teachers who receive on-going staff development to learn to work with
Different learning styles and diverse cultures
They need teachers willing to come out of their comfort zone to experience other cultures

They need teachers understanding the "Have To" Black students experience everyday
They need teachers who look like them
They need teachers who do not only teach them the way they learn but have many
Instructional strategies to use understanding that students learn differently
They need teachers who integrate their history and contributions throughout their curriculum

Ebony Thoughts

They need teachers who are not afraid to nurture
and challenge them at the same time
They need teachers to understand how their history
and ancestral history has presented
Many obstacles on equal opportunities and access

They need teachers who acknowledge their own
isms and seek out ways to address them
To be a better teacher

They need teachers who are trustworthy, genuine,
challenging, experienced, risk-takers,
Inclusive, culturally responsive, and welcoming that
believe all students can achieve and are Willing to
put in the extra effort needed to reach and teach
their students and save them from
Drowning

Ebony Thoughts

Why Does It Hurt So Bad?

When we look at history
African Americans endured so much pain
Through slavery, mistreatment, and our time in history
The feelings were unbearable
As a people, we were not taught about the major accomplishments and contributions
Our ancestors made
We were not taught the brilliance of our people
Many times, it appeared we had no history beyond slavery
We had an invisible history
We were never taught otherwise
Sometimes we closed our eyes to not see the treatment of our ancestors
We denied that African Americans or any human being could be treated so badly
And with such malice

When movies were made or books were written about our history
It was unbearable
Movies such as Roots, Rosewood, Mississippi Burning, Martin Luther King, Jr., Malcolm X
Brought a jolt of reality to our history
Sometimes as a people we chose not to acknowledge
This part of our past because it provoked anger and deep levels of resentment
And for some shame and self-hatred

Ebony Thoughts

We were not taught to be proud by the perpetrators
In spite of it all
Our ancestors instilled in us self-pride
Some at a major cost
Many died to get an education
To free their family and
To revolt against injustices

Why does it hurt so bad?
When others deny their entitlement and privileges
because of the color of their skin
The feelings of superiority
The denial that their ancestors wronged a whole race of people
The denial that their ancestors could savagely treat another with blind rage
And justify such treatment.
They denied emasculating our men, raping our women, and dismantling our families
African Americans must learn their history
Acknowledge the bad and ugly we experienced
And know that there is good and strength in our people
That we are a proud people, a resilient people, and an accomplished people
That even though we had less we had more than others
That we are religious, spiritual, and strong willed people
That despite it all we are survivors
We must accept our past
Take the strength from our ancestors and
Embrace our present and

Ebony Thoughts

Grow from these experiences so we can have
A future of hope, achievement, and become stronger
Provide a source of pride so
It won't hurt so bad for future generations

Time - Make Every Second Count

Moves Continuously
Without interruption
Stays still for no one
Cannot be negotiated
Cannot be paid to end
Not controlled
It epitomizes equal opportunity
Does not discriminate
Moves with ease
Tick tock, tick tock, tick tock
Does not stop
We control what we do with our time
Make every second count

Mama's Boy

Tall, dark, and handsome
Son, a mother's dream
Busy, inquisitive, outgoing, shy, funny, smart
Development of brilliance
Mother's pray for them as they grow
Up against the odds
Teach survival skills, a way of life

Birth
A moment of joy and sadness
Joy for the wonderful boy who will become a great man…
Son, father, grandfather, role model
Sadness because of society's images and history's lessons about
The Black male, misunderstood, labeled, abused, stereotyped, genocide
Negative images in abundance

Mama's boy
Makes you laugh, cry, and proud
Laugh at their stories as they go through the various phases of manhood
Cry when you see their pain and you can't take it away…a part of the growing process
Proud to be his mama

Ebony Thoughts

Proud to see him grow from mama's boy to a strong, intelligent, kind, gentle, supportive,
Responsible, spiritual, and resilient man of substance
Proud to see him be a husband, father, a rock for his children …A Mama's Man

Educate Not Incarcerate

Education is
A means to an end
Our way out
We must know from whence we come
To know where we are going

Appreciate the past
Painful as it is
Sacrifice, blood, sweat, and tears
Strong, determined, relentless
Spirits soar through it all

As a people, we must stand tall
In spite of it all
Our stock is high
For education, many of our ancestors have died

Our contribution is plentiful
But to some our history is meaningless
Brothers and sisters
Wake up, we cannot sleep anymore
For many doors that were opened, many have closed

No longer be a prisoner of fear
Plot your path and go liberate your
Mind, body, and soul
We must be bold

Do not let others plot your destination

Ebony Thoughts

We are the captain of our ship
The more we know the further we will go
Knowledge is power

Education is the key
Unlock your cell full of anger, hopelessness,
Distrust, fear, jealousy
Do not feel incarcerated

Use the key of education and make a difference
Lift yourself up and your brothers and sisters
Together we are no longer prisoners
But free to change, to uplift, to grow, to challenge,
To learn, to educate
We must educate our people
Not to be incarcerated by ignorance
We are our own gatekeepers…

Rise

down
falling further in
trying to stand
weighted by demons
holding you still
not moving
slowly you make progress
floating to the top
rising above pain, hurt, bad judgement, and demons
seeing the light

The Mask

The face shows
What you want to see
But is that person
Really me
The smile, the look, the joy, the sound
Deep down inside it's really a frown
You see what you want to see
The mask shows a part of me
Look deeper and you will see
Who's really inside
The real me

Through the Eyes of Babies

God's gift to parents
To love, guide, and mold into productive citizens
Babies are innocent
Not aware of the world around them
Open to new ideas
They see people as one
Do not discriminate
Because of the color of one's skin, race, creed,
national origin, and religion
They are like sponges
Soaking up knowledge
Eager to learn
They need unconditional love
Their eyes sparkle with the excitement
Of their next adventure
They bring joy, love, and hope
Babies fill voids in our heart
As adults, we need to view life
Through the eyes of babies
Seeing their innocence
And imparting love to those in our presence

A Season of Hope

A Season of Hope
Allows us to grow, believe
And know through sheer determination
You can experience and survive the changes of life
Hope allows us to see
The future where possibilities exist
It helps us to forget the
Pain of the past and know life can improve

Hope allows us to heal
And see the joy
Hope helps us to believe in ourselves and others
It lets us know that through
Trials and tribulations there is light at the end of the
Tunnel
Hope allows us to see the best in ourselves
And forgive mistakes we've made in the past
It helps us to get up in the morning
And face a new day

Hope lifts us up when we fall
Not allowing us to stay down
But to stand tall
Hope challenges us to think
Beyond the moment
And see the future
Hope allows us to see
During our darkest hours
That this too shall pass

Ebony Thoughts

Hope will lift you high and
Not allow you to fall into the abyss
A ray of hope shines bright and is electrifying,
 Shocking us to new heights and will not allow us to fall into harm's way
But through God see a better way
A season of hope is ongoing
Allowing you to change with life's circumstances
Lifts your spirits when you are down and
Keeps you believing through your faith

Ebony Thoughts

This was one of the first poems that I read at a spoken word event. I was inspired to write it after all of the events that happened around the election of President Barack Obama, the first African American President of the United States. Now, in 2017, many of the elements that are present in this poem are still relevant today.

The More Things Change the More They Stay the Same

The more things change, the more they stay the same
History has a way of repeating itself
Where progress was made
Much has been lost
The experiences of the past can be painful
To the core of your being
Some wounds are hard to heal
And some never will
They are deep and will leave a scar
But through it all we go on
We fight, we compromise, we co-exist, we succeed
Thinking that life will be better for our children
We pray that they never experience the pain, alienation, and feeling of not being worthy
And the hatred bestowed upon our ancestors because of the color of their skin
We must never forget the blood, sweat, and tears they endured to ensure
A better life for us
We are a resilient people
When attempts were made to break our
Spirit, control our minds, and plant the seeds of doubt
We excelled in spite of it all

The more things change, the more they stay the same

Ebony Thoughts

Our people had to march, protest, and stand their ground
So we could get an education
Be provided equal opportunities to find employment, vote, be treated with respect
Be seen as a human being, not less than an animal
Slavery planted many seeds of self-hatred, self-doubt, and led to
Post traumatic slave syndrome
Racism continues to raise its ugly head
Spitting the venom of hatred, prejudice, and division of racial and ethnic groups

We must not forget the Little Rock Nine, Linda Brown and Brown vs. the Board of Education, Hank Aaron, Jackie Robinson, Muhammad Ali, Arthur Ashe, Althea Gibson, South Carolina State Massacre, Marian Anderson, Rosa Parks, just to name a few
Who stood their ground making inroads for future generations

The more things change, the more they stay the same
Let's fast forward to now when we have many of the same struggles
Now-We have Jena 6
Now-We have Barry Bonds
Now-We have the reversal or dismantling of affirmative action
Now-We have a conservative Supreme Court that is making decisions that will have
Ramifications for the future

Ebony Thoughts

Now- We have segregation in many schools
Now-We continue to have unequal funding for education
Now-We have our Black boys assigned disproportionately to special education classes
Now-We have marches for equality and justice
Now-We have many incidents of police brutality
Now-We have a court system that has a dual system of justice
Now- We have the media that reports news that is biased against people of color
And is equivalent in the pain inflicted in the past

The more things change, the more they stay the same
We must develop policies that will support equal opportunity,
Educational advancements, funding equities, health care for all, justice for all
And not let it be threatened by the sign of the times

Find Your Wings

Sometimes in life we
feel we are falling and unable to fly
Because life happens
And we feel broken

This is the time we must test our faith
Reach for hope to keep us stable
Trust God because he has a plan for us
We may not know what it is
But God will show us the way

We may struggle to hold on
Trying not to fall
Looking for balance in our life

As time goes on we become stronger
Not letting fear of failure or disappointment stop us
We look back at those experiences and lessons that
were learned

Through these trying times
We find our way and
Are now ready to soar

We find our wings and fly
To our next adventure
We know that with God's guidance
We will survive

Black Girls Lift Your Head High

Black girls lift your head high
Above the negative images displayed about you
The offensive words used to describe you
The stereotypes that those in power choose to
continue to use to put you down

You are above that
You are a survivor and strive
Despite efforts to keep you down, lower your self-
esteem, and devalue your beauty
Embrace your body, nose, lips, hips, eyes, size, hair,
And shades of ebony
Love the skin you are in

Black girls lift your head high
You are here for a purpose
Embrace your uniqueness
Love yourself, respect your body, and demand
Respect
Embrace your gifts, your history, and your future

Black girls lift your head high
Knowing that God makes no mistakes
And he made you

The Box

A box has four corners
And is enclosed at the top
It can be full of faith, hope, love, joy, peace, long suffering, and temperance
Or
It can be full of hate, rejection, fear, discrimination, prejudices, and negative myths
It can possess tools of success
That can take you a long way
Or
It can hold instruments of oppression
That will have a negative stay
The box can be full of knowledge
And have staying powers
The box is like a person
It can have a top and bottom
It is full of possibilities
What will you put in your box?

Young People Wake Up

Young people wake up
And take the challenge before you
You are our future
And that can be frightening
Not only to you
But to everyone
You have so much potential
There are no limitations to your future
But you
You can rise beyond the peer pressure,
unemployment, teenage pregnancies, gangs, drugs
And other ills that are out there
To steer you in the wrong direction
Making good choices is part of living
Wake up young people
Because the choices you make
Will impact on your future

Silence

A voice with no sound
Speaking but not heard
Screaming and shouting
Wanting to release
No one's listening to the cry
Life continues to move on
Existing in a bowl
Slowly your voice is heard
Silence turns to sound

A Ray of Hope

Let not life's circumstances dim your light
Of
What could and can be
Believe
That you deserve all that's offered if you put out
equal effort
Continue to believe in your potential
Never question your capability
Strive for excellence
Believe in yourself
Believe in your future
Believe in who you want to be
Do not let others dim your light
Let it shine bright
Because
There is always that ray of hope

Ebony Thoughts

What's Race Got to Do With It?

What's race got to do with it?

For those who are disenfranchised, voiceless, not valued, experienced prejudice and inequalities in funding, redlining, lack of health care, unequal education, and experienced isms,
Race has everything to do with it

When you experience racism because of the color of your skin, your culture, your uniqueness, and differences
Race has everything to do with it

Those who are discriminated against because of these factors have a heightened sense of awareness and are alert to these injustices
Those who are privileged, empowered, and are not discriminated against because of the color of
Their skin or their race is least aware of these injustices

We must see through the eyes of those who are affected, the impact it has on them
As an individual and their race
When your voice is silenced, your history invisible, stereotypes define you, your intelligence is
Questioned and freedom isn't free or equal
Race has everything to do with it

When your children don't love themselves because all they see, hear, or learn about their culture is negative. They have low self-esteem and negative attitudes about their race because they are not exposed to the positive and not taught their history or about the valuable contributions of their race Race has everything to do with it, so let's do the right thing....

Let's acknowledge the injustice of the past and work to right the wrongs of the past
Let's move forward in our quest for equality and social justice
Let's acknowledge and embrace the beauty of the rainbow that reflects the beauty of diversity
Let's empower all youth by teaching pluralistic history and not monoculture history
Let's empower our youth in the beauty of differences not the negative of diversity
Let's take a stand for change and make a difference in the present and future and learn from our past

What's race got to do with it? EVERYTHING! Make it count by doing your part to impart mutual respect, equal opportunity, embracing the uniqueness and beauty of all cultures, and taking a stand for social justice. If significant changes are made, diversity is valued, history is equal, injustices no longer exist, and racism is a thing of the past. Then when asked this question, "What's race go to do with it?", the answer will be..."NOTHING!"

We Are Our Own Worst Enemy

Black People Wake Up
We have been enslaved for so long that the effect
still clouds our judgement
We were taught not to trust each other
To believe that anything by Whites was better than
our own
We were taught to hate each other and feel inferior

Wake Up Black People
We must not make it our business to pull each other
down but to lift each other up
We can agree to disagree while at the same time
fighting for a common cause that will
Help our people
We must not be our own worst enemy
Looking for the bad and ugly
We must look for the good

We must not be like the crab
Pulling those who are progressing and successful
down
Afraid that one day they might have more than you
We must push those individuals upward
They stand on the strong shoulders of our ancestors

Those of us who are moving forward
We should not forget from whence we come
We must not forget our brothers and sisters who are
still struggling
We must reach back and lift them up

Ebony Thoughts

Sharing our experiences, knowledge, resilience, and fortitude

Black people we must learn to not use words to stifle our peoples' growth
If you don't have anything positive to say about your fellow man
Then it might be best to say nothing at all
Words are like knives and they can be very hurtful
And you cannot take them back
So use them wisely

We complain about the negative stereotypes
But many times we are the ones to enforce them
Wake Up Black People
We must learn to not be our own worst enemy
But be our own supporters
Because at the end of the day we are all we got

Proud Black Woman

Beautiful
Shades and shapes undeniable
Lips full and luscious
Striking curves
That accentuate the body
Features created to show the beauty of the Black
Woman

Hair
Natural, curly, straight
Beautiful coarseness that's unique and
Shows personality

Women of character, grace, and poise
Dignified in times of oppression
Strong in times of rejection, abuse, and injustices

History has not been kind to the strong Black
woman
Who has been subjected to rape
Children taken and sold
Men and husbands dehumanized
Separated from her family
Abused, degraded, and many times made to feel less
than human
Like an object without feelings

Through her faith, will, and desire to be who God
made her to be
She takes her gifts to provide for her family
Love and support her man

And raise her children to become loving and caring human beings

The proud Black woman
Despite all she has endured
She has survived
To rise beyond the negatives
Acknowledging her past
Becoming stronger because of the sacrifices of Black women before her
Looking forward to the future with faith, anticipation, and hope

Ebony Thoughts

This poem, "The Alpha Woman", was written in 2008 when Alpha Kappa Alpha Sorority celebrated it's centennial (1908-2008). As an AKA woman, I was inspired to write about what Alpha Kappa Alpha means to me and my sorors. It was my honor to write this poem for such a memorable occasion.

The Alpha Women

Alpha represents the beginning
Alpha Kappa Alpha Sorority is the first African American Greek Sorority providing guidance for other sororities that followed
The Alpha Woman represents women of character
She is strong, loving, nurturing and intelligent
The Alpha woman is dedicated to the causes of the sorority
The Alpha woman is a civil servant, she gives of herself to strengthen her family
And the community

The Alpha Woman is the rock of her family, her community, and is a leader
She wears many roles-wife, mother, grandmother, sister, auntie, and friend
The Alpha Woman does not put any man before God, herself, and her children
The Alpha Kappa Alpha woman strengthens the sorority through strong sisterhood
And a sense of purpose

The Alpha Kappa Alpha woman wears the colors of pink and green to show pride
And showcase the beauty of Alpha
The Alpha Woman is a woman of character, grace, and poise
Dignified in times of oppression
And strong in times of rejection, abuse, and injustices

Ebony Thoughts

The Alpha woman teaches her daughters that
despite efforts to keep them down,
Lower their self-esteem and devalue their beauty
Embrace their body, nose, lips. hips, eyes, size, hair,
and shades of ebony
Love the skin you are in
The Alpha woman teachers her daughters to respect
themselves, their bodies, and to strive to be Women
of character and not to settle for
Less than a man of substance
They teach their sons to respect women, how to
become a man of substance, and how to survive.

The Alpha Kappa Alpha Sorority has shown
longevity, fortitude, and strength
By continuing to grow despite challenges and
celebrating its
Centennial –1908-2008…100 years of Alpha

The Alpha Kappa Alpha women are confident, giving, leaders, organizers, planners, women of character, philanthropists, supporters, family oriented, community supporters, role models, educators, and mentors. They serve in many roles to catapult the sorority and the next generation of sorors to the next centennial.

A Mother's Touch

As a child, we are taught many things
How to tie our shoes.
How to use the bathroom.
How to properly wash our hands.
How to put on our clothes.
How to eat a healthy meal.
How to speak.

This is taught with unconditional love by our mothers
Mothers have the touch to make the sore hurt less
Make food taste better
Make the long road trip seem shorter
Mothers sometime have eyes in the back of their heads
They see your mischief
And you wonder, how in the world did they know?
They discipline you
While loving you none the less

Mothers request that you get involved in activities
That will help you grow
They do this sometimes without your say
And you want to say no way

As time goes by and you excel in your activities
You say thank you for being the adult
Thank you for saying yes when I said no
And thank you for saying no when I wanted you to say yes

Ebony Thoughts

They run from one event to the next tired
And patiently waiting for you to finish
And with a smile on their faces and internally exhausted
They take you to your next event

A mother's love is irreplaceable
A mother's touch is forever
It is gentle, loving, guiding, and firm
All at once
Making you into the wonderful adult you are

Ebony Thoughts

See the Beauty in Me

Many times we see our flaws
More vividly than anyone else
My stomach is flabby and not so tight
My thighs are thick and not quite right
My bottom jiggles just a little bit
And sometimes is flat when I sit
My muscles in my arms have disappeared
And my breast has decided to take a rest
My eyes are small and big and bright
My hair is black, blonde, red-oh what a sight
I can't go out, no not tonight
I am too tall and can't find a date
I am too short and why is my date late
I see myself in the mirror
My reflection looks at me
And you know what?
I like what I see
I see the beauty in me

In Her Shoes

Walking in the shoes of phenomenal women
All styles, shapes, sizes, colors, cultures, religions
Unique to each woman
They are the foundation to our frame
Carrying all the load we have to bear

As women, we have characteristics
That are as unique as we are
We are loving mothers, wives, sisters, aunties, and
Friends
We love our children and spouses unconditionally
We value our family
We wear many hats, chauffeur, cheerleader, doctor,
Friend, role model, caregiver, supporter, lover,
Comforter, teacher, educator, mothers, believers,
Provider…to name a few

Life throws many challenges at us
And some are harder to overcome than others
But through our faith, determination, creativity,
And resiliency we survive
When we look at life
And our stories, we wear them well

Shoes comes in all styles, shapes, costs, colors, and
sizes and fit the personality of the women
Who wear them
They accentuate the beauty of the women
Providing them with the support
To move forward in life
And striding with their head held high

Ebony Thoughts

And confidence to take on a goal
The beauty of women shines through from the
Inside and out and their stories are unique to their
Life circumstances, struggles, successes, families,
Obstacles, and socio-economic status

In your shoes you should love who you are
See the beauty in you and
Acknowledge your strengths to overcome
challenges and become the beautiful woman you are

Black Child

Black child
The fruit of a rich vine
Grounded deep in history
Has a unique story to tell

Full of substance
Resilient and strong
Striving in spite of shackles
Strong in the face of being denied
The same opportunities to flourish
Nourished with the blood of the ancestors

Black child
Full of life and dreams
Excelling despite struggles and challenges
Rooted in a strong people
A strong history

Black child
Loved unconditionally by the family
Guided by life's lessons, God, and the belief
That he/she too is worthy, brilliant, and he/she can make a difference

Black child
Who will be the vine, the root and the substance
For the family
Guiding future black children to not believe all the negative images about them
And how to be a leader and overcome adversity

Ebony Thoughts

Black child
You are the light
Shining bright
Making inroads for the future
Leading you to grow, face challenges, make good decisions, and be a unique individual
Continuing to strengthen your past, present, and future

Claflin University-You Are One Of A Kind

Claflin University
You are one of a kind
Touching the lives of many Black students
Challenging them to succeed
Imparting knowledge, a sense of purpose, cultural pride, and confidence

You believed in us when others didn't
You did not see us as failures, deficient, or incapable of learning
You saw the brilliance in us
You saw the potential
You ignited the spark

You taught us about our history
You taught us to love ourselves
We no longer have an invisible history
But a proud history
Our voices were heard, not silenced
And we lifted them higher

You touched me as a student
Many years ago
When I was going through the era of Jim Crow and segregation

I was fighting to be educated
Fighting to be heard
Fighting to belong
Fighting for my rights
My energy was slowly being depleted

Ebony Thoughts

But, you gave me hope
You revived my soul and spirit

You allowed me to be a student
I didn't have to fight to belong
You embraced and guided me
You taught me about our ancestors who died for us
So that we could have a better life
And who made tremendous contributions to make this country great
You taught me to be a better person
And provided me the needed nurturing, guidance, and instruments of excellence

Through Claflin, I felt like the burden of the world had been lifted off my shoulders
And I could breathe and believe in myself and my future
I could be a student
Free to learn without distractions
You gave me a ray of hope that life could be good
You provided me with the tools I needed to get a terminal degree
You bestowed upon me the foundation to go anywhere and succeed

So, I say to you Claflin University
Thank you for believing in me
Thank you for the keys of education
Thank you for filling my mind with knowledge
And giving me the edge needed to compete
Thank you for seeing my potential

Ebony Thoughts

And preparing all your students to face the world
And step up to the challenge
You are one of a kind

Believe In Yourself

Believe in yourself
You are worthy
You are capable
Believe in who you are, where you want to go
And know you will reach your goals
Do not let others define you
Limit your potential and
Break your spirit
Life is full of ups and downs
Highs and lows
It's up to you how you handle these difficult times
in your life
You can let self-doubt rule
And stay down, waddling in sorrow
Or
You can let hope lift you high
Push you beyond belief and
Closer to your dreams
Knowing the process requires you to
Crawl, walk, and then run
With your head held high
A stride in your walk and
Confidence in who you are

Believe in yourself
Even when others don't
When you are told you can't reach your goal
Use this as a challenge to propel yourself into action
Because action speaks louder than words

Believe in yourself

Ebony Thoughts

Love yourself
Challenge yourself
The more you believe in yourself
The more you will achieve
Knowing that life is full of challenges, fears, and restrictions
Embrace your potential
Embrace your gifts and
Believe that you will SUCCEED

Not Good Enough

Try Hard
Work 110%
Do your best
But
You are not good enough

Believe in yourself
Set high goals
I will decide your future
Because
You are not good enough

Get a good education
Work harder and smarter
However you don't fit in
Because
You're not good enough

Do not let others
Break you down
Devaluing your hard work
Silencing your voice
Standing in judgement of your best effort

Think smart
Work hard
Believe in yourself
And know
You Are Good Enough!

Finding Our Voices

Free speech
Sharing our thoughts, beliefs, and goals
For our future and our family
Rejoicing at life's opportunities
That are available to us
Believing that we the people can make a difference
Praising God, lifting up our voices
Believing that life is good

Circumstances suggest otherwise
Poverty, miseducation, racism, economics
Silencing a peoples' dream
Silencing a peoples' voice

Rejoice we must
Making our voices heard for our people
Finding our voice to express
What we as a people want

Finding our voice to make decisions that will
impact on our people
Finding our voice in spite of circumstances,
hardships, inequalities that make us silent

Open our minds, our soul, and free our voices
That they may be heard for the betterment of our
people

Dream the Possible

To dream the possible
You must believe
You must dream it
To receive it

Many of us do not dream
Because we believe the impossible
We are told we cannot achieve it
We are not encouraged to dream
Beyond our realities

Some of our realities limit our dreams
We do not have food in abundance
A roof over our heads may be mobile,
There are no guarantees
Education provides us possibilities
But opportunities are not always equal

We must encourage our children
No matter their life circumstances
They must not limit their goals
But be bold beyond their imagination
Because they deserve the best

They are worthy regardless
Poverty should not limit their dreams
Naysayers should not limit their dreams
They need to be exposed to the possibilities
And encouraged to dream the possible

Pain

Pain
Sharp
Deep
To the core
Bottled up but cannot open
Deeper, inside and out
The emotion is closed
It's hard to expose
Turning, churning, oozing as it implodes
Out with a sigh
Hurtful no lie
Ease, relief, slowly opening up from inside
Pain no more

Self Doubt Can Hurt

Self-doubt can hurt
It can deter you from reaching your goals
It can limit your outcome
Cause you not to believe in yourself

Many times it can be negative self-talk
Making you question why you should be blessed
You don't deserve this break
No one will support your efforts
It's not good enough

Self-doubt can hurt
It can keep you down
Discouraging you to believe
And put out the effort
Needed to succeed

Many times it is ingrained deep
In your being
Causing you to be your own worst enemy
To see the worst versus the best
In what you've accomplished

Self-doubt can be changed to confidence
Change negative self-talk
To positive self-talk
Believe you are worthy
And accept your blessing
When given a compliment
For touching someone's heart
Say thank you

Ebony Thoughts

Know God gave you the gift
To help others see the light, to believe

Self-doubt can hurt
Both self-confidence and believing in yourself
Can take the hurt away
And help you to grow
Positively everyday

Strive for Excellence

Strive for excellence
Challenge yourself to go the extra mile
And not settle for less
But to always do your very best
Life is full of roadblocks
Confront each hurdle
And use it as a challenge to reach higher
When you are faced with difficulties
Know that is part of life
You must figure out a way to get around the problem
To move beyond the dilemma
And advance to the next level
Knowing you will face barriers
Life is an obstacle course
It has many twists and turns
It's how you play the game
That will make a difference
Work hard, don't quit
Embrace challenges and Disappointments
Know you are strong and have inner strength
Believe and
Strive for excellence

Behind the Curtain

Behind the curtain provides us privacy
A time to reflect on what has happened
In the past, present, and look to the future
It is also a time for introspection
To see what really matters to you
To assess your values, beliefs, hopes, culture,
Community, family, political views, and the world

It covers the mask that you wear
It allows you to take off the cover
To not have to wear your public face
It allows you to expose the real you
Your private thoughts that only you know

Many go behind the curtain and
Expose a side of themselves
That is not very appealing
They show racial prejudices, sexism, age discrimination, classism
Religious bias, ethnocentrism, deceit, personal conflict
And things about themselves
They do not want others to know

Decisions that are made behind the curtain
Can have a profound impact on the future
Do not hide behind the curtain
Do not be afraid to open up to possibilities
Rise to the occasion and
Make a difference

Why Me?

Why Me?
Why not me!
For God determines what's right you see
I must keep the faith
When I'm feeling down
And find a way to turn it around
Why me? Why not me!
Only God knows what the outcome will be
But you have the power
To choose eternity

Ebony Thoughts

I was asked to submit a poem for the magazine Community Strong for Thanksgiving in 2014. I did not have a Thanksgiving poem at the time. I thought about all my blessings and how fortunate I was. We all have a lot to be thankful and grateful for. These blessings inspired me to write the poem, "Count Your Blessing".

Count Your Blessings

We all have blessings that are a part of our lives
The ability to wake up and see another day
The ability to see the beauty of God's work
To hear sounds of our environment and nature
To speak words of encouragement and
Communicate with others
The joy of being with our family and friends
Food to nourish our bodies and share with our loved
Ones, a lifetime partner to share our love
A roof over our heads for shelter and comfort
The opportunity to give back to our community
The thrill of meeting a goal we've set for ourselves
The ability to see the light during our darkest hour
And hope for a better day and peace around the
world

The willingness to choose hope over hate during
Tumultuous times in our country
The ability to dream the possible
The capacity to love unconditionally
The aptitude to learn
The fortitude to provide guidance, values, and
Support for our children
The optimism to believe in the possibilities and not
Be afraid of challenges
The strength to not let fear rule our actions and stop
Us from living
But face our fears
With zest and zeal for life

Ebony Thoughts

This time of year touches our hearts in so many
Ways
It allows us to enjoy the moment and reflect on the
Past
It allows us to smile as we think of our loved ones
No longer with us
We have so much in which to be thankful
Life, love, happiness, health, friends, family,
Accomplishments, compassion for others, and God
In our lives

Share your gifts to impact on the life of someone in
Need of hope
Who may be in pain, feel hopeless, alone, alienated,
And not worthy
Use your compassion to make a difference in the
Lives of others
Keep your faith, embrace, and share your bounty
Be thankful for your life's circumstances and
Count your blessings

Ebony Thoughts

The Historical Plight of the Strong Black Man

How do you describe the Strong Black Man?
He is all shades of ebony, handsome, and
Has intelligence in abundance

History has not been kind to our Black men
Despite all the humiliation
Efforts of emasculation
Being treated worse than an animal
Devalued and hated
Our Black men are still standing

Many endured more pain
Than any human being should be allowed to feel
They were put in a position
Of enduring humiliation
As a survival mechanism
They watched their women and daughters being raped
Children sold to the highest bidder
And themselves sold to the highest bidder
Because of their size not their minds
They were murdered because of the color of their skin
Not because they committed a crime

Our strong Black men
Worked hard in the fields
Threatened constantly for being rebellious
Many were killed for looking at a White woman
They walked with their head bowed because

Ebony Thoughts

If they looked in the eyes of a White person
They could die

When we look at slavery
We look at the injustices
Our people endured
But none as inhumane
As the treatment of Black men

Many lynchings occurred because the Black man
Stood up for his rights, his family, and his people
Many occurred because the White man had the power
To destroy a life, not having any guilt
Because they viewed him as nothing but a "nigger"
And they were the justice system
Hatred was paramount during this time
White children were taught to hate Blacks
To see them as beneath them
That they were not to be respected
But they expected Black adults and children
To respect them because of their race
They were taught their race was superior
And provided them privileges, entitlements and
They emulated their parents

Black men were acknowledged for their athleticism
Humor, music, and dance
Not their intelligence
They were taught they were not smart,
Not handsome, self-hatred, not worthy of an education,

Ebony Thoughts

To be servants, to serve the White man, to be docile,
To endure humiliations
Not seen as a human being
Entitled to rights of dignity, protection, support their family,
And all civil liberties

Our Black men were smart
They taught our Black boys how to survive
They taught them how to play the game
And fight for change
They taught them that Whites can
Abuse, humiliate, and treat them disrespectful but
They can't take away your mind and soul
Our Black boys were taught
How to become Black men

We salute our warriors
Our protectors, our strong Black intelligent brothers
The development of this country was built on
The blood, sweat, and tears of our ancestors
Today many of the same injustices still apply
Our strong Black men
Still have to struggle
Endure a dual justice system
Live with the impact of past injustices
Not treated as equals and
Having to still prove themselves despite many achievements

They are loving husbands, fathers, grandfathers, brothers, and uncles

Ebony Thoughts

That are teaching their sons how to be a man
Black boys have three strikes against them at birth
They are Black babies
They are Black boys and
They will be Black men
We must not allow their spirit to be broken
But teach them how to survive and become
Responsible, resilient, intelligent, spiritual
And strong Black men

Ebony Thoughts

I wrote this poem in November, 2008 when the nation elected our first African American president, President Barack Hussein Obama. It was so monumental in history. I never thought in my lifetime that I would see an African American president. His cadence during the election was, "Yes We Can". It motivated me to write the poem, "Obama, Yes We Can". The poem highlights the HOPE he was bringing to America and the pride he was bringing to African Americans. He stood on the shoulders of greatness, our ancestors, to reach his goal.

Ebony Thoughts

Obama-Yes You Can

Obama-yes you can
Bring about positive changes
That will impact on the nation and the world
The more things change, the more they stay the
same, however, you have brought about changes in
beliefs, in hope, in unity, in a nation that has been
widely divided across race, religion, socio-
economic status, and gender
To name a few

Change is an action many find hard to make
They are comfortable with the status quo
And see life through rose colored lenses
When their life is shaken up and the unfamiliar
occurs, many emotions come to surface
Some that are not so positive
Never in my lifetime did I ever
Expect to see this change in our nation
This ray of hope
That an African American male would be
Nominated as the Democratic nominee for
President of the United States of America

When I think about our forefathers
The pain, hurt, degradation, alienation,
And inhumane treatment they endured
Just to be treated like a human being
Change is Good

Ebony Thoughts

When I see my high school son come home after hearing your acceptance speech for the Democratic Party nomination and he says he wants to recite your acceptance speech when he does forensics in the fall
Change is Good

When I see my daughter, a college student
Engaged in the political process and say, "Mom I got there just before 8:00pm but I voted.
I participated in history"
Change is Good

When I see my husband
Who is a historian reflecting on major events in history?
The good, bad, and the ugly
Discuss challenges you have faced and will face
With the media, conservatives, and naysayers
Beaming with pride to see your accomplishments
Change is Good

When I hear, my young nephew say he is glad to see a brown man run for president
That lets him know he can be president too
He can dream the possible
I say change is good

Ebony Thoughts

When I see a nation discussing the silent dialogue of race and having healthy and unhealthy conversations about an uncomfortable topic
Change is Good

As with anything else in life
Being a change agent isn't easy
You will not win everyone's support
Because there are those with ingrained isms
Continue to believe in yourself
Stick to your goals
Keep your faith
Weed out negative comments, commentaries, and the media
Look ahead because where history has been made
There is more to come

Because YES YOU CAN!!!

Impulse

Sometimes we make decisions
On an impulse
On the spot
In a moment's notice
With little thinking about consequences
Impulses can be good and bad
Good when you react on something
That will positively affect your life
Bad when it's based on your mood
Which may not support the outcome
Impulses can bring many outcomes
Let your impulses bring
Positive results to your life

Keep the Faith

Sometimes in life we make choices
That have negative consequences
The punishment can sometimes seem harsh
But despite it all life goes on

The circumstances you are experiencing are not ideal
But you have to make the most of your situation

Take this time to reflect on
What you've done
What you have learned and
Where you plan to go from here

The thing about life experiences, good or bad is
There is always a lesson to be taught
You must learn from your decisions
If it was a good decision, you may want to do it again
If it was a bad decision, you must learn
To not repeat it and reflect on what you would do differently

Know that there are people
Who believe in you
Who love you and
Who want the best for you

Keep the faith
Keep believing in yourself
Know that life can be better for you

Ebony Thoughts

Everyone deserves a second chance
Make Yours Count!

Toxic People

Negative aura
A snake waiting to strike
Leaving its prey in harm's way
Not blinking, not moving
Still

Looking for a conquer
At any cost
Cannot be trusted
Only concerned for self
And to hell with others

See themselves as a gift
That others covet
Wanting to be like them

Steer yourself away from
The snake, with toxic venom
Do not allow yourself to be in striking distance
Allowing the venom to enter your system
Life is too short.

Ebony Thoughts

Why Teach? Why Not!!!

Teaching is one of the most powerful professions out there
The impact on the life of students is for a lifetime
It is relevant for all professions
Because we must learn our craft
And teachers teach
Teachers can motivate students to learn and challenge themselves
Or
They can break their spirit and discourage them from dreaming and reaching their goals

We need teachers who embrace the diversity students bring into the classroom
We need teachers who see the gifts and talents students bring into the classroom
They don't focus on the deficits but the strengths
We need teachers who are willing to put out
The extra effort to help students learn
We need teachers who have high expectations for all students
Not believing that because of life circumstances they cannot learn

We need teachers who use a variety of instructional strategies to reach their students
Knowing all students learn differently
We need teachers who know learning is a lifelong adventure
They seek professional development to grow

Ebony Thoughts

We need teachers who love teaching
Not see it as a means to an end
We need teachers who are passionate about their profession
We need teachers who see the value of the student's culture
They encourage their students to value their past, present, and future
We need teachers to recognize the power they have in the classroom
They use that power to empower all students not to break them down

We need teachers to see the brilliance and the resilience students exhibit
We need teachers who are risk-takers and understand the "Have To" many students bring into the classroom
We need teachers to infuse multicultural education in all aspects of the curriculum starting as early as kindergarten
We need teachers who are nurturing, creative, and caring

We need teachers who can engage the students and not use the sit and get methods all the time
We need teachers who are passionate about imparting their knowledge
We need teachers who help all students find their voices not silence them
We need teachers who see the value of collaborating with the child's parent, community, and other significant individuals

Ebony Thoughts

Why Teach, Why Not!!!
Teaching can change your student's life forever
In a positive or negative way
Teach to propel your students to learn, to believe, to set, and reach their goals
And know that teachers are change agents and we are all learners

Do Not Let Life's Circumstances Limit Your Outcome

Some people are blessed with material riches, opportunities for success are a part of life's expectations. They are privileged to have their basic needs met...employment, health care, education, food, and housing. They go to the best schools, take the most rigorous college preparation classes, they are taught by highly qualified teachers who have high expectations for them, and they attend summer camps or precollege programs. Their future is set and it's up to them to take what is given to them and make their future better.

Others are products of poverty, food is not promised, a roof over their heads is not guaranteed, unemployment, single family household, living paycheck to paycheck, disappointments, and failure are a part of life, no medical services are available, and violence is a part of their daily being.

Their children attend schools where some teachers don't believe in them, they have low expectations for the children, many are not highly qualified, and work for a paycheck-not the dividend of making a positive difference in the life of a child. Children are told to take high school classes that will not prepare them for college but for minimum wage jobs, and they do not attend summer camps and precollege programs...the streets are their summer opportunities.

Ebony Thoughts

Despite these circumstances, these children have what it takes to be successful. History has shown that many students who are products of families with less means have triumphed and been successful despite life's negative curve and many with the means and the foundation have failed despite having the best of everything.

We must teach all our children that despite life's circumstances, positive outcomes are available to them.

Fight Everyday We Must

Black
Beautiful and blessed
Misunderstood and labeled
Why
Because of the color of our skin
Beautiful and brown, almond, black, and caramel
Shades undeniable
Black and proud
Yes indeed
Rights denied
Opportunities denied
Fight everyday we must
Taught to feel inferior
Invisible history
Resilient people
Strong, determined, brilliant, passionate, survivors
Fight everyday we must
We wear the badge of color
Tan others seek to acquire
God's gift to us
Fight everyday we must
For our children, our ancestors, and ourselves

Ebony Thoughts

Don't Break Their Spirit

Our little Black boys are our gems
They will grow into great men and loving fathers
But many are not allowed to explore
The many steps between childhood to manhood
Not because of their gender
But because of the color of their skin

Our little Black boys have three strikes against them at birth
They are Black babies, they are Black boys, and they will be Black men
We must not allow their spirit to be broken!
They need guidance and opportunities to be who they are

They must have teachers who embrace them, not fear them
They must have teachers who are not threatened by their style, size, skin
Color, or voice
They need teachers who will not try to silence their voices but hear what
They have to say
They need teachers who see their gifts and talents and
Not see them as special needs
Because they are high energy and need movement

They need teachers who do not assign special education labels because they
Learn differently

Ebony Thoughts

They need teachers who see the brilliance in them and allow that light to
Shine bright
They need teachers who embrace their differences, challenge and not fear
Them but believe in their capabilities

They need teachers who have high expectations of them
Letting them know failing is not an option
They need teachers to see them as the individuals they are, not based upon
The negative images that are in abundance about them
They need teachers who will not break their spirit but strengthen their
Foundation, hear their voices, embrace their differences, and encourage their
Spirits to soar

Ebony Thoughts

This poem was written when Barry Bonds was approaching breaking his own homerun record and striving to hit 800. There was an accusation that he was on steroids and this was never proven. Baseball had an ugly stain on its image and record. Many pitchers chose to walk him to avoid him breaking the record. He received death threats and hate mail. I remember his young daughter begging for the pitchers to pitch the ball to her father. It was a negative time for baseball and America. This is what inspired me to write the poem Barry Bonds Go-756.

Barry Bonds-Go 756

We as a people are so proud of Bonds'
accomplishment
As children, we are taught to set goals
To go that extra mile to become the best we can be
To believe that no matter the color of your skin
Every man can be successful
History, however, has also taught us a different
lesson if you are Black man

As a Black man you have three strikes against you
at birth
You are a Black baby, you are a Black boy, and you
will be a Back man
And the justice system is not always equal as it
relates to Black men
Bonds' accomplishments are not tarnished
We have been taught that in America
You are innocent until proven guilty
That's the American way if you are White
However, different standards apply if you are Black
Every man should be given his day in court
To prove he is innocent or be convicted of a crime
When proven guilty
This has not been the case with Barry Bonds
The mantra for him is he is guilty until proven
innocent

Where is the justice?
Shadow of suspicion does not mean guilt
Race is a divide in this country
When there is an issue that has a racial overtone

Ebony Thoughts

There is usually a racial division
If you ask many Black people, they are proud of
what Bonds has accomplished
It gives a ray of hope
If you ask many White people, many will say he is
guilty and doesn't deserve
The title of best hitter in baseball history

History has a way of repeating itself
Let us not forget Hank Aaron
Another great Black hero
He was not accused of committing a crime
His only crime was being a Black man on the brink
of breaking
The coveted record of Babe Ruth, a White icon
He received death threats from racist fans, hate
mail, and racially charged media coverage
Not because he was not the best hitter at that time
worthy of breaking
And surpassing the record of Babe Ruth, but
because of the color of his skin
Isn't it amazing that thirty-three years later, Bonds
is being subjected to the same treatment, only
With more intense scrutiny

Let us also not forget that the commissioner during
that time did not feel that it was worthy of
His presence to attend this historical game
Does this sound familiar?

So I say to Bonds, "You have inspired a new generation to strive for the impossible like you were inspired by Willie Mays, Hank Aaron, Jackie Robinson, and most notably your father Bobby Bonds". I say Barry, "Do not let them break your spirit, continue to rise above the negative, and bask in the moment. You've earned it. Congratulations!"

Ebony Thoughts

I wrote this poem in 2009 during President Barack Obama's first term as President of the United States. An ugly side of America raised its head. Many racists began to show their faces and incite hate. This faction disrespected our President. They removed their masks and became vocal about their views of racism. A racial divide began to grow in our country. I wrote, "Here We Go Again", because it felt like we were going back in history to the time of segregation and the Jim Crow Era. White supremacy groups started getting a voice through their conservative movement. Hate and anger was beginning to get a voice over HOPE.

Here We Go Again

History has a way of repeating itself
We reflect back on what has happened in the past
The good, bad, and ugly
And recently ugly has lifted its head high
Many people now are hiding behind health care, economy, struggling educational systems, dysfunctional families, and the demise of the housing market to justify their hidden feelings of racism because the more things change the more they stay the same

We have been blessed to see an African American President
And for some they believe this proves racism doesn't exist
However, many negative groups are using this monumental time in our history as a way to justify their actions
To be disrespectful to our President of the United States of America

For many with limited vision
They feel it is okay for them to come out
To take off the mask they have worn to hide their true feelings about an African American man leading this country
They believe it is alright to go to town hall meetings
And yell not discuss issues that affect our country
Resembling mobs of the past

Ebony Thoughts

Inciting fear by bearing arms citing the second amendment at what is supposed to be a peaceful event
Trying to dishonor our President by calling him a liar and dishonoring the Congress
While millions watched in shock

If we are allowed to disrespect our President
Then other countries will feel they can do the same
It sends an erroneous message
We as a nation set the tone
They believe they can go on TV networks and rationalize these behaviors
This country is heading in the wrong direction
Going back to the times of segregation and White supremacy
They do not respect the office of the presidency
Because they do not believe an African American man can be intelligent and make decisions that will propel this country in a new direction

Many of these conservatives are angry
And hate is taking over
They use politicians and other conservative talk shows
To wake this faction
To energize racism in America
To incite fear of change
They encouraged those in the past who hide behind the hoods to come into the light
We are going through a bad time in this country
When we let these racists have a face and voice
Wake up America!

Ebony Thoughts

We cannot go down this road again
Where we feel justified to be disrespectful, hateful,
and feel our race makes it right
It's time to show pride, patriotism, and unity
The actions that will make America proud
We cannot go back but move forward
Because if we are to survive as a nation
We must agree to disagree
While doing the right thing
Moving our country in the direction of change
We all can be proud of
We ALL must do our part to keep America great!!!

Ebony Thoughts

This poem was written in 2001. I received my doctorate in Counseling Psychology with an emphasis on Counseling Students of Color from Marquette University in 1992. My dissertation topic was, "Meeting the Needs of African American Students on Predominately White Campuses". As we approached the 21st Century I was motivated to write, "Being an African American Student in the Twenty-First Century", based on my experiences as a Black student on White campuses and my research. Many of the issues found in my research continue to resonate for African American students today on White campuses.

Being An African American Student in the Twentieth First Century

Being an African American student means seeing very few African American students in the classroom. In many instances continuing to be the only one in the classroom.

Being an African American student means to continue completing a degree program and not having an African American professor. Seeing very few African American advisors and counselors.

Being an African American student means having a stronger appreciation and knowledge regarding your leaders past and present.

Being an African American student means continuing to be exposed to negative attitudes and doubting Thomas's who believe you are not capable of doing as well as your White counterparts

Being an African American student means you must continue to be super students juggling isolation, activities, academics, racism, financial need, social estrangement, and lack of resources and being expected to have a meaningful college experience like your White peers.

Being an African American student means you must continue to get lip service about change but little action

Ebony Thoughts

Being an African American student means you are all viewed as the same versus being viewed as individual students with various needs

Being an African American student means continuing to have your history viewed as unimportant to the point that it is not taught as part of the overall curriculum where all students can benefit and having African American instructors teaching the class. It means continuing to be an invisible culture.

Being an African American means still not having African American counselors in the counseling, career, admissions, financial aid and housing offices to whom you can relate and trust and who understand your concerns

Being an African American student means continuing to educate administrators about your needs and seeing very little change take place over the past 30 years.

Being an African American student means being judged negatively because of displaying African American pride through my attire, kente cloth and scarves, braids, music, hair, celebration of Kwanzaa, etc. Being viewed as radical because of your cultural heritage.

Being an African American student means being viewed negatively as a troublemaker, criminal, drug dealer, rapist, or murderer if you are an African American male.

Being an African American student means continuing to be isolated, needs ignored, frustrated, challenged, displayed, prejudged, subjected to low expectations for success, and not provided the opportunity to be a well-rounded student like your White peers.

Ebony Thoughts

This poem was written in 2012. During this period, President Barack Obama was running for his second term as President of the United States of America. Hate groups increased, race relations became more turbulent, and citizens' rights to vote were being challenged. Roadblocks were being developed, i.e., voter identification requirements to threaten voters right, especially voters of color. This inspired me to write, "It's Your Choice: Hope or Hate" because we, as American citizens, had to make a choice behind the curtain. The season of hate was raising its head.

It's Your Choice: Hate or Hope

We are going through a difficult time in our country
We have a mood of unrest, uncertainty, and
negative changes that are occurring
This can impact a nation, negatively

Many changes and policies that were enacted to
right some wrongs of the past are being challenged
Many people who were disenfranchised in the past
from voting
Are now being faced with state policies that will
take away their right to vote,
Equal access to opportunities and affordable
healthcare

We have hate groups now that feel they have the
right to openly discriminate
Against an individual because of race, religion, and
sexual orientation
We have individuals who feel they can disrespect
our President because
He is a Black man

We have a political party whose whole agenda is to
not re-elect President Barack Obama
By any means necessary
Not because he is not qualified
But because of the color of his skin

Ebony Thoughts

We are now living in and experiencing a Season of Hate
This existed during the Jim Crow era in the south and racial segregation
Many of these racists now have a voice through the Tea Party
And other hate groups

As Americans we have a choice…HOPE or HATE?
We must choose equal rights for everyone
We must choose to not disenfranchise voters
We must choose to fight against those who believe in hate
Because of one's race, religion, or sexual orientation

We must choose high quality educators for all students
We must choose affordable health care
We must choose peace over war
We must choose to help the poor, unemployed, and homeless
We must choose freedom of speech
We must choose equal rights
We must choose equal protection from law enforcement
We must choose women's right over their bodies
We all have a choice to make…what will you choose?

Ebony Thoughts

I wrote the poem, "Michael Jackson: A Journey of Greatness" after his untimely death. This is my tribute to the King of Pop, Michael Jackson. He was a musical genius who crossed cultural lines. He advocated for social justice, the environment, and making the world a better place.

Ebony Thoughts

Michael Jackson: A Journey of Greatness

Michael Jackson touched the hearts of many
Through his music, dance, and humanitarian work
He was known all over the world
Addressing issues such as racism, poverty, love,
healing the world, the earth, and family
He started so young on this journey of greatness
He sang as a young boy to a man with passion that
would draw you to his music
His dance moves were legendary
They have been duplicated all over the world
He is truly a legend
That was loved by many
He was also a father
Who loved his three children
He wanted to provide them the childhood he was
denied

He had to grow up to soon
To make adult decisions and face challenges most
kids his age were not exposed to
To this end, he cherished the idea of being young at
heart
To live his childhood dreams at Neverland
His own dreamland that allowed him to live out his
childhood as an adult
Michael loved his family and fans
His biggest fan was his mother
Whom he held in high esteem

On June 25, 2009

Michael Jackson left this earth too soon
We may never know why but God has a plan for each of us
Michael lived his life to the fullest
And like all of us made mistakes
Despite it all he touched the lives of many
Through his kindness, soft spoken voice and his generosity
Michael is being remembered as a man who could and did make a difference
He shared his God-given gifts that touched our hearts and mind

He was a believer, perfectionist, father, family man, friend, philanthropist
And world class entertainer
Who had to wear the mask
Fearing many would not accept him for who he really was
We saw his public face but his private face was very different
He was loved by many but he also was a lonely man
Not knowing his impact on the world
He will live on through his music, videos, movies, family and friends
Michael Joseph Jackson
Rest in peace
Continue to entertain in the great beyond
As you embark on your new journey

About the Author

Dr. LaVerne Jackson-Harvey has over thirty-five years of experience in K-12 and postsecondary education in counseling, advising, research, teaching, public speaking, and program design. She started writing her poetry at a late, but exciting time in her life. She has authored over 200 poems. Dr. Jackson-Harvey published two books of poetry entitled *Life Circumstances: Do not Let Life Circumstances Limit Your Outcome* and *A Ray of Hope*. Recently, she published a children's book entitled *Ruth and Her Hoots*. She received her bachelor's degree from Claflin University, master's degree from Bowling Green State University, and doctorate from Marquette University.

Ebony Thoughts

While employed at Marquette University, Dr. Jackson-Harvey founded The Night of Black Literature, a program that allowed students and staff to read their favorite poetry by African American authors. She has read her poetry at numerous events. She is the wife of Robert L. Harvey and they are parents of three children, Dalila Granger, Rashida Harvey, and Gary Harvey. Dr. Jackson-Harvey was raised in Inman, South Carolina and lived in Milwaukee, Wisconsin. Currently, she resides in Charlotte, North Carolina.

www.ingramcontent.com/pod-product-compliance
Lightning Source LLC
Chambersburg PA
CBHW071008160426
43193CB00012B/1964